Ghosts
and Ghouls

by
David Orme

Thunderbolts

Ghosts and Ghouls

by David Orme

Illustrated by Jeremy Long

Published by Ransom Publishing Ltd.
Radley House, 8 St. Cross Road, Winchester, Hants. SO23 9HX, UK
www.ransom.co.uk

ISBN   978 178127 077 6

First published in 2013

Contents

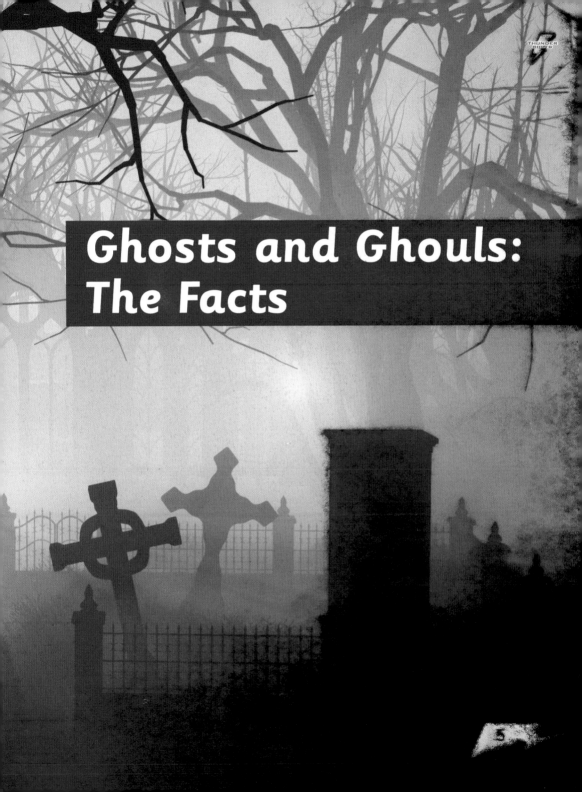

Ghosts and Ghouls: The Facts

What is a ghost?

Is it ...

The spirit of a dead person?

Something we can't explain?

Something that just isn't true?

What do you think?

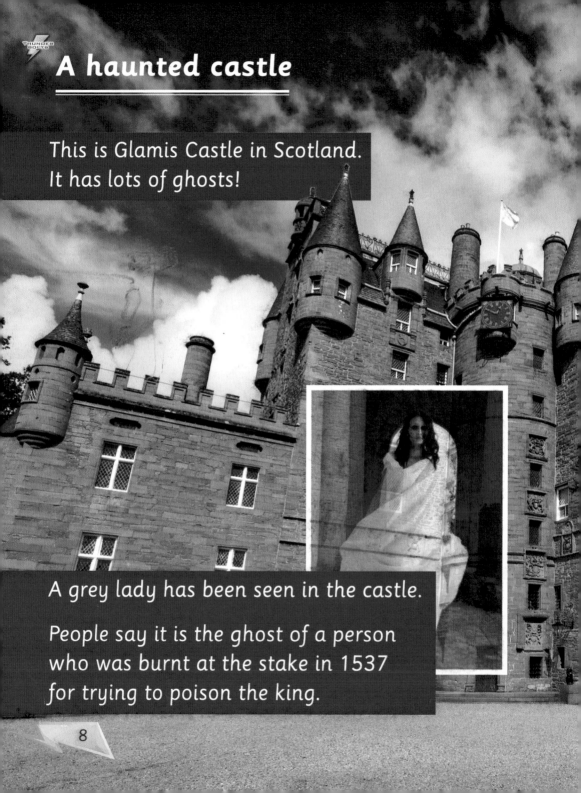

A haunted castle

This is Glamis Castle in Scotland. It has lots of ghosts!

A grey lady has been seen in the castle.

People say it is the ghost of a person who was burnt at the stake in 1537 for trying to poison the king.

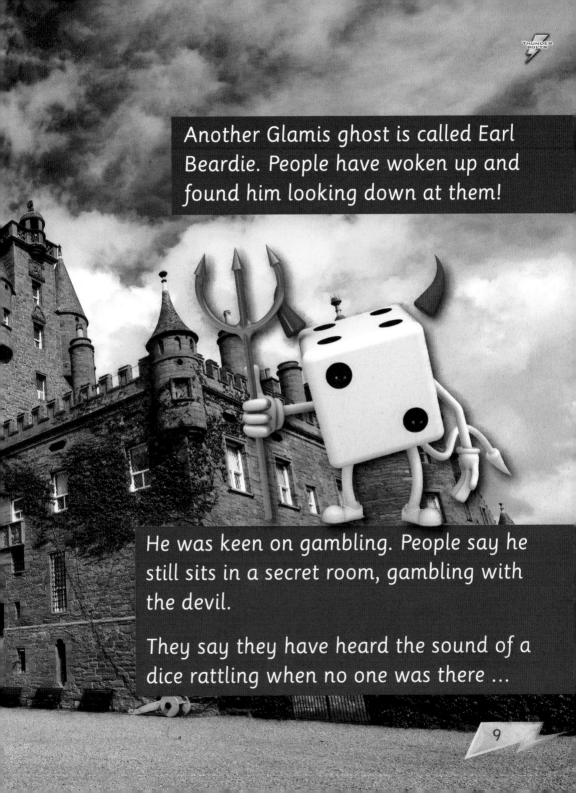

Another Glamis ghost is called Earl Beardie. People have woken up and found him looking down at them!

He was keen on gambling. People say he still sits in a secret room, gambling with the devil.

They say they have heard the sound of a dice rattling when no one was there ...

A screaming skull

This is a house called
Bettiscombe Manor.

There is a human skull in this house.
It is the skull of a servant.

When he died, he was buried in the
churchyard, but he didn't like it
there. People heard screams
coming from his grave!

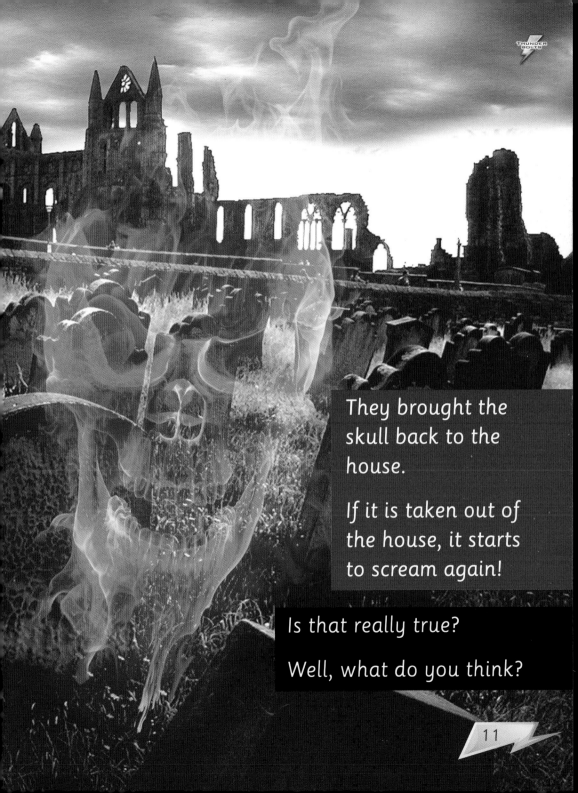

They brought the skull back to the house.

If it is taken out of the house, it starts to scream again!

Is that really true?

Well, what do you think?

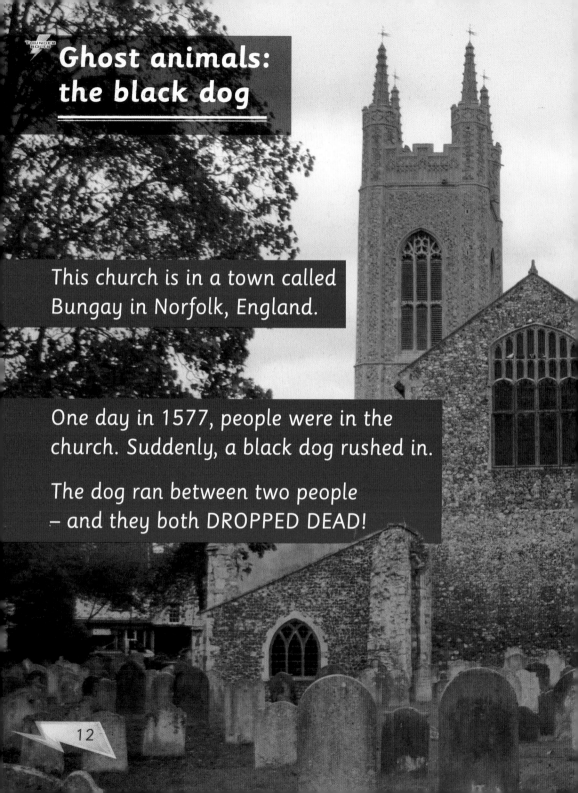

Ghost animals: the black dog

This church is in a town called Bungay in Norfolk, England.

One day in 1577, people were in the church. Suddenly, a black dog rushed in.

The dog ran between two people – and they both DROPPED DEAD!

People say that if you see the ghost of a black dog it means bad luck.

Does it?

Well, it was for those two people in the church!

Ghost armies: a haunted battlefield

This is Sedgemoor, England.

A terrible battle was fought here in 1685. You can still hear the sounds of marching feet and galloping horses.

You can hear a woman crying. The man she loved was killed in the battle.

She drowned herself in a pond.

Can you really hear these sounds?

You'll have to go there and listen for yourself!

Ghost ships

The Mary Celeste

The Mary Celeste was found sailing along … with no one on board!

What had happened?

Pirates? Aliens? Something scary that made them jump overboard?

No one knows!

The Flying Dutchman

Some sailors say they have seen a ghost ship at sea. It glows with a weird red light.

What's the story?

The crew of the Flying Dutchman did something evil. Their punishment is to sail the sea forever.

So it's still out there?

Well, possibly.

Painting 'The Flying Dutchman' by Albert Pinkham Ryder

What is a ghoul?

There are lots of stories about ghouls.

They are creatures that are not alive ...

... but they are not dead either.

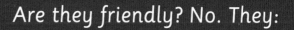

Are they friendly? No. They:

- live in graveyards

- grab children who are passing by and kill them

- eat dead bodies.

Here are some other creatures that are not alive or dead:

a vampire ... a werewolf ... a zombie.

Are any of these stories true?
Just come into my graveyard and I'll tell you ...

The day of the dead

In Mexico every year there is a 'day of the dead'.

On that day people remember friends and family who have died.

People dress up and make sugar skeletons and skulls.

20

They visit the graves of the dead to leave gifts for those who have died.

People take the dead people's favourite food and have picnics at the graves.

They hope that the souls of their dead friends will visit them and grant their prayers.

So are ghosts real?

Is this a real ghost?

Yes!

Because lots of people have said they have seen them.

More than one person has seen the same ghost.

There are even photographs of them.

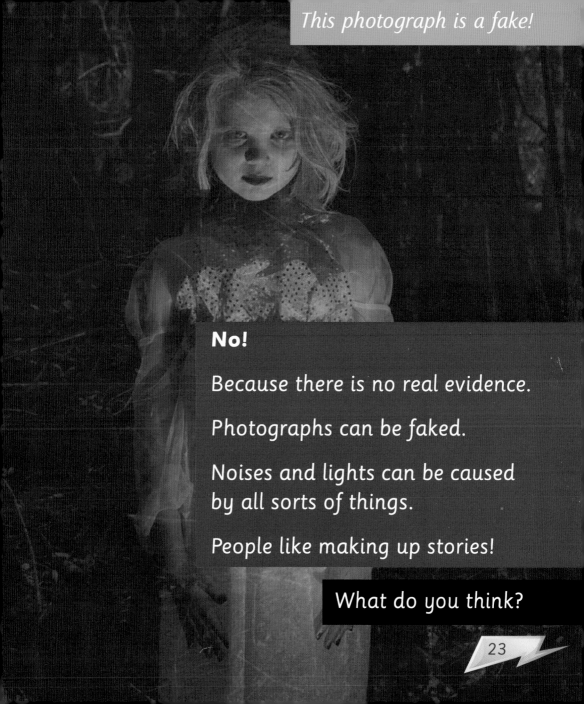

This photograph is a fake!

No!

Because there is no real evidence.

Photographs can be faked.

Noises and lights can be caused by all sorts of things.

People like making up stories!

What do you think?

23

The Haunted Hotel

Dan and Tasha's uncle was telling them a ghost story.

'That hotel is closed now. I worked in that hotel. People said Room 13 was haunted! It was the ghost of a boy who died there.'

Dan and Tasha didn't believe it, but when they walked past next day they saw something surprising ...

Dan and Tasha decided to explore.

Round the back they found an open window, and they climbed in.

The inside of the hotel was very spooky!

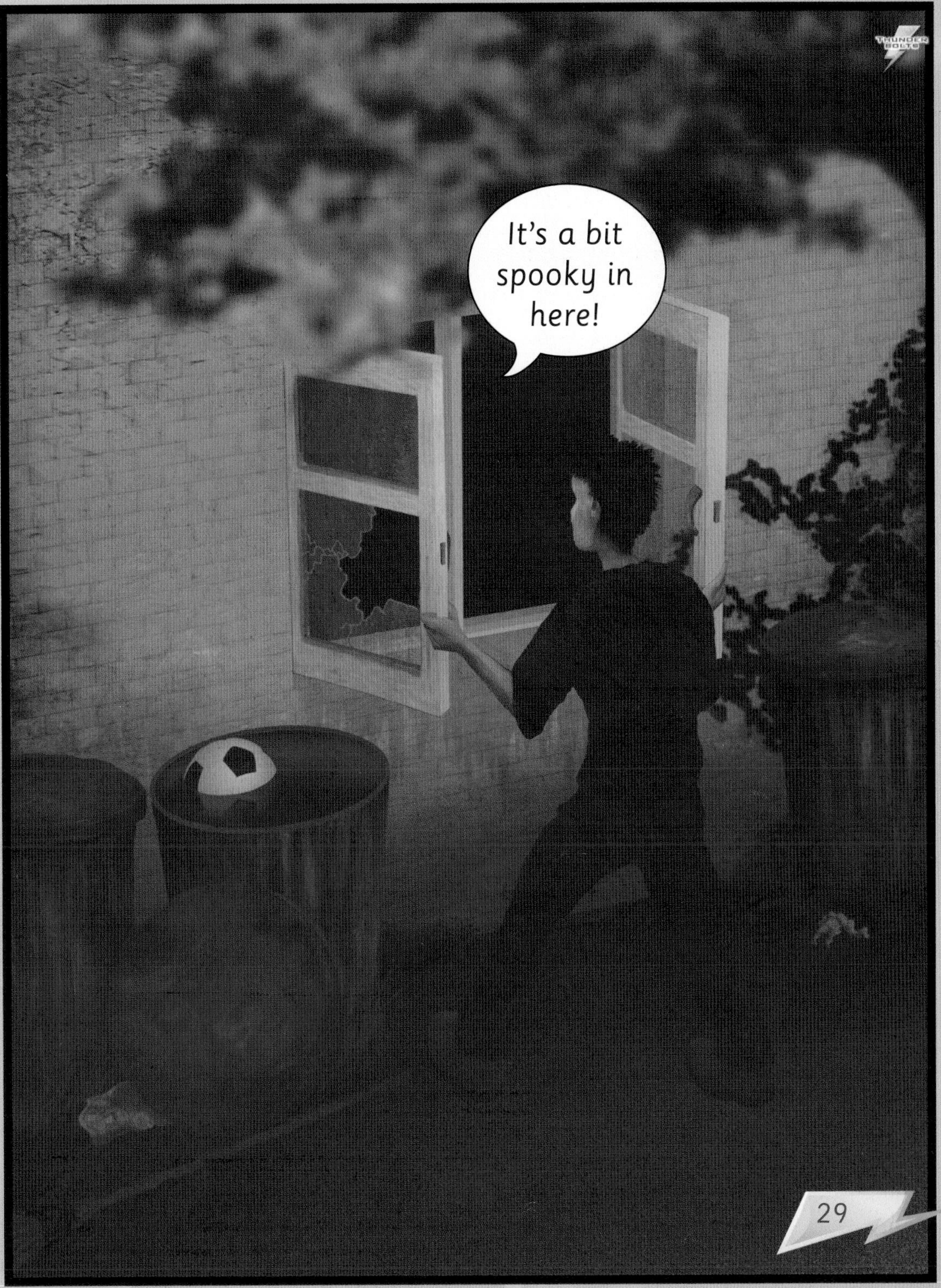
It's a bit spooky in here!

They headed up the stairs to look for Room 13.

From inside the room they heard a voice. It sounded like a young boy shouting for help!

The door was jammed.

Dan ran at it and forced it open.
Inside was a small boy.

He told them that he had been
exploring and the door had got stuck.

Tasha rang for the police.

Then the police and the boy's parents arrived.

They were very grateful to Dan and Tasha.

'You must have been really frightened,' Tasha said to the boy.

'I wasn't frightened at all,' said the boy. 'I found a friend in the room, and he talked to me … '

Word list

battlefield
evidence
graveyard
haunted
light
Mexico
noise
photograph

punishment
scream
skull
spirit
vampire
werewolf
zombie